AXIS PARENT GUIDES SERIES

A Parent's Guide to Teen FOMO

A Parent's Guide to Influencers

A Parent's Guide to Instagram

A Parent's Guide to TikTok

A Parent's Guide to YouTube

A Parent's Guide to Teen Identity

A Parent's Guide to LGBTQ+ & Your Teen

A Parent's Guide to Body Positivity

A Parent's Guide to Eating Disorders

A Parent's Guide to Fear & Worry

A Parent's Guide to the Sex Talk

A Parent's Guide to Pornography

A Parent's Guide to Sexual Assault

A Parent's Guide to Suicide & Self-Harm Prevention

A Parent's Guide to Depression & Anxiety

PARENT GUIDE BUNDLES

Parent Guides to Social Media

Parent Guides to Finding True Identity

Parent Guides to Mental & Sexual Health

A PARENT'S GUIDE TO
SEXUAL ASSAULT

A PARENT'S GUIDE TO

SEXUAL ASSAULT

Tyndale House Publishers
Carol Stream, Illinois

Visit Tyndale online at tyndale.com.

Visit Axis online at axis.org.

Tyndale and Tyndale's quill logo are registered trademarks of Tyndale House Ministries.

A Parent's Guide to Sexual Assault

For information about special discounts for bulk purchases, please contact Tyndale House Publishers at csresponse@tyndale.com, or call 1-855-277-9400.

Library of Congress Cataloging-in-Publication Data

A catalog record for this book is available from the Library of Congress.

ISBN 978-1-4964-6762-1

Printed in the United States of America

29	28	27	26	25	24	23
7	6	5	4	3	2	1

I always wondered why survivors understood other survivors so well. Why, even if the details of our attacks vary, survivors can lock eyes and get it without having to explain. Perhaps it is not the particulars of the assault itself that we have in common, but the moment after; the first time you are left alone. Something slipping out of you. Where did I go. What was taken. It is terror swallowed inside silence. An unclipping from the world where up was up and down was down.

CHANEL MILLER, *KNOW MY NAME*

CONTENTS

A LETTER FROM AXIS

Dear Reader,

We're Axis, and since 2007, we've been creating resources to help connect parents, teens, and Jesus in a disconnected world. We're a group of gospel-minded researchers, speakers, and content creators, and we're excited to bring you the best of what we've learned about making meaningful connections with the teens in your life.

This parent's guide is designed to help start a conversation. Our goal is to give you enough knowledge that you're able to ask your teen informed questions about their world. For each guide, we spend weeks reading, researching, and interviewing parents and teens in order to distill everything you need to know about the topic at hand. We encourage you to read the whole thing and then to use the questions we include to get the conversation going with your teen—and then to follow the conversation wherever it leads.

As Douglas Stone, Bruce Patton, and Sheila Heen point out in their book *Difficult Conversations*, "Changes in attitudes and behavior rarely come about because of arguments, facts, and attempts to persuade. How often do *you* change your values and beliefs—or whom you love or what you want in life—based on something someone tells you? And how likely are you to do so when the person who is trying to change you doesn't seem fully aware of the reasons you see things differently in the first place?"[1] For whatever reason, when we believe that others are trying to understand *our* point of view, our defenses usually go down, and we're more willing to listen to *their* point of view. The rising generation is no exception.

So we encourage you to ask questions, to listen, and then to share your heart with your teen. As we often say at Axis, discipleship happens where conversation happens.

Sincerely,
Your friends at Axis

---

[1] Douglas Stone, Bruce Patton, and Sheila Heen, *Difficult Conversations: How to Discuss What Matters Most*, rev. ed. (New York: Penguin Books, 2010), 137.

REAL TALK ABOUT SEXUAL ASSAULT

WE ALL PRAY that our children will experience a world safe from harm. We do our best to love and protect, but what do we do when things are out of our control? Sexual assault is a serious and scary thing, and we need to talk to our kids about it. As parents, we should equip our kids and ourselves with practical tools to prevent the unthinkable.

The National Center for Victims of Crime reports 1 in 5 girls and 1 in 20 boys is a victim of child sexual abuse.[1] If our children haven't experienced abuse, chances are they've got a friend who has. So it's our job to learn how to love our kids through it if they've experienced it firsthand—and to prepare them to be a good friend to victims of abuse.

WHAT IS SEXUAL ASSAULT?

SEXUAL ASSAULT is any form of sexual contact or behavior that occurs without the consent of the victim. It's a big umbrella term that includes much more than rape—it can be attempted rape, uninvited touching or fondling, forcing the victim to perform sexual acts, or any other case of unwanted physical contact. Above all, it is *never* the victim's fault.

Sexual assault usually falls into one of three categories:[2]

1. Penetration crimes

2. Contact with intimate body parts

3. Exposure of intimate body parts

Each state varies slightly in its definition of what sexual assault is, but when it comes down to it, there is no excuse for unwarranted sexual acts.

HOW DO I TALK ABOUT IT WITH MY KIDS?

IT'S NEVER TOO EARLY TO DISCUSS SEX, boundaries, and consent. Start these conversations when your kids are young so they know it's all right to bring these topics up. The key is to adjust your tone, specifics, and level of depth based on your child's age.

One of the best ways to start a conversation is to look for organic opportunities to do so. Pay attention to the media, video games, YouTube videos, or even stories from school that your child tells you about. Actively search for ways to generate conversation between you and your child. If your family watches something on TV that shows some form of sexual assault, ask your child for their opinion on what happened. Or if they see a post on social media that discusses the topic, use their technology to relate with them. This can lead to a more natural discussion of a rather tough topic.

But it's also important to address the topic directly and intentionally. It's easy to assume that if our kids are under a certain age or if they haven't brought it up with us, they're simply unaware of it and everything is fine. But the truth is, that's often *not* the case. When it comes down to it, most (if not all) parents would agree that they'd much rather have awkward conversations that either prevent assault from happening or help their kids come to them first than have painful, heart-breaking conversations *after* something terrible happens and regret not bringing it up sooner. So it's crucial to talk openly about sexual assault *before* something happens.

When you bring it up in conversation, talk about not only what sexual assault is but also warning signs to look out for. Many young people can't conceive that people they know may have bad intentions, let alone recognize inappropriate things as they're happening (more on this later in the booklet). Though sad, it's important to bring up the fact that 93 percent of victims know their perpetrator.[3] It could be a friend, a classmate, a relative, or someone else they trust. Making sure our children know about the reality of sexual assault is the best thing we can do for them because it gives them the ability to look out for themselves. And if talking about it feels awkward, that's perfectly all right! These conversations are tough. Let your kids see your humility about the subject.

In addition, it's important to talk to your kids about loving others who have experienced sexual assault. Most people don't know what to say or do when a friend comes to them with a story of abuse. First, tell your kids what an honor it is for

When you bring it up in conversation, talk about not only what sexual assault is but also warning signs to look out for. Many young people can't conceive that people they know may have bad intentions.

a friend to disclose that to them. Help your child understand how much a friend must trust them to share that information. This can also show your child that you have confidence in them to do the right thing when talking with a victim. Encourage them to use language of love and support with their friend, like this:

- "Thank you for telling me about this."

- "I'm so sorry that happened to you. You did not deserve it."

- "I am always here for you."

It's vital to teach our children how to love others well, because that's what God calls us to do. Proverbs 17:17 gives a great example of strong friendship. Show your child that community is a powerful tool that God's given us to lift each other up in

times of trouble. Friends love at all times—
especially when someone's been hurt.

Part of this love should typically involve
notifying a trusted adult about the incident. Even if the friend wants it to remain
a secret, reporting it to someone who can
help will make it less likely that others
will experience assault by the same
perpetrator.

HOW DO I PREVENT IT?

A QUICK NOTE: A CHILD'S ASSAULT is *not* the fault of poor parenting or lack of preventative measures. The only one to blame is the offender. That being said, there are ways to help prevent sexual assault from happening.

TALK ABOUT CONSENT.

Our kids need to know what it means to give consent and what appropriate boundaries should look like. *No means no—end of story.* We talked about this a bit earlier, but let's dive in. We need to start these conversations young so our kids understand that they have control over their own bodies. No matter who it is, if someone is uncomfortably close or begins to touch in an inappropriate way, no means no. Clearly define consent for your child so they can be prepared if a situation arises where they need to use firm language or defy an authority figure. Because many assaults occur in a relationship where one party has power or authority over the other, equipping your children with the courage and permission to resist abusive authority figures is critical to their ability to understand and confront an abuser.

Consent is verbal permission to do something. If this is not present, then it's assault. Consent is *not* assuming that a person's clothing or behavior condones sexual activity with them. We need to make sure our kids—especially our girls—understand that there is never an excuse for an assault against them. If drugs or alcohol are involved, there was not consent. If they were pressured into something, there was no consent. Assault is not their fault. We must make sure our boys understand that there is never any justification to take advantage of a girl,

A child's assault is not the fault of poor parenting or lack of preventative measures. The only one to blame is the offender.

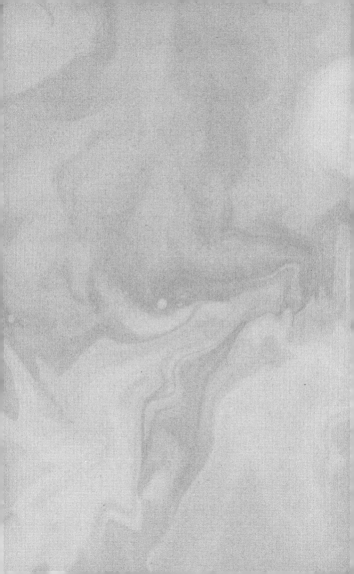

especially if she's made choices (drinking or drugs) that make her unable to consciously object to sexual activity. Encourage your sons to be protectors of the vulnerable, not complicit bystanders.

Of course, we want to encourage our children to stay clear of situations that could leave them in a vulnerable place. But the truth of the matter is, sexual assault can happen anywhere. Our kids should know that without verbal permission, the offender has no right to continue. Let's help our children—girls and boys alike—understand what consent *is* and *is not* so they can treat others with respect.

BE A SAFE PLACE.

Part of being a safe place is creating a safe space for our children. If our homes are safe and comfortable, our kids will be more likely to open up about difficult subjects. Openness and honesty must be important parts of the culture of our homes. *As parents, we want our children to know that no matter what they do or say, they are loved and heard.* If we're a safe place, our kids will know that they won't be penalized for telling the truth.

One key way to love our kids well is by making time for them. Set aside a few minutes each day without any distractions (i.e., phone nowhere to be seen) to ask about school, their friends, and their emotions. Take interest in their interests. We have to create an open space for communication so that when more serious issues take place in our kids' lives, they immediately know to whom they can turn. Finding the balance between friend and parent can be tricky, but it starts with caring about the little things.

Clearly define consent for your child so they can be prepared if a situation arises where they need to use firm language or defy an authority figure.

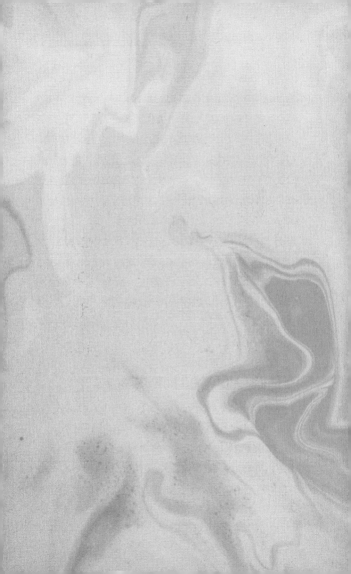

If we're a safe place for our kids to come to, we can look out for warning signs with clarity. This could mean seeing when a boyfriend becomes controlling or forceful over time, noticing adults who get too close to our children, hearing about social gatherings or parties that could be unsafe, or learning about any other concerning situation. Don't be afraid to discuss difficult topics. When we're a safe place, nothing is off the table, and our kids will know that we won't react out of fear or anger—but out of love, protection, and wisdom.

ENCOURAGE YOUR CHILD TO TRUST THEIR GUT.

If something seems off, it probably is. This can start with everyday happenings like roughhousing between siblings that goes a little too far, playful teasing among friends that turns hurtful, or a social gathering that makes them feel uncomfortable. We want our kids to know that if they're feeling uneasy, it's completely valid to leave. If they know that hurtful words are unacceptable, they'll be more likely to recognize when something's gone too far. If they know "lighthearted" teasing is never an excuse for inappropriate touching, they can be empowered to leave a compromising situation immediately.

We need our kids to trust their gut because those emotions often point to real danger. Sometimes a gut feeling may actually be the Holy Spirit prompting them to flee from troubling circumstances or moving in a subtle way that notifies their bodies that something isn't right. Teach your children to recognize and pay attention to these promptings. If you have examples from your life when you experienced some sort of internal

Our kids should know that without verbal permission, the offender has no right to continue.

prompting, describe exactly what that felt like. That way, our kids can then look out for themselves and others when something just doesn't seem right.

HOW DO I EQUIP MY CHILDREN TO AVOID ASSAULT?

TALK TO YOUNGER KIDS ABOUT . . .

- **The names of their body parts.** Teach your kids proper names so they can feel comfortable asking questions.

- **Which body parts are private.** God made their whole body special, but some of those parts are for their eyes only.

- **Saying no.** Kids grow up knowing that they are supposed to obey adults. When talking to your kids about private parts, let them know that it's okay to refuse any form of contact. Teach them the "No! Go! Tell!" strategy.[4] Say "no" firmly to inappropriate touches, get away, and tell a trusted adult.

- **Not keeping secrets from you.** Let your child know that they

can always be honest with you—
especially if someone has told them
to keep something a secret or if
they think they'll get in trouble for
speaking up. In fact, you'll be proud
of their honesty no matter what,
even if they confess something
they've done wrong.

TALK TO OLDER KIDS ABOUT . . .

- **Looking out for themselves.**
  Our kids often think nothing bad
  can really happen to them. Teens
  feel invincible: danger always
  happens to other people, not to
  them. Talk about the importance
  of boundaries and knowing how
  to respond if a boundary is crossed
  before things go too far.

- **Healthy relationships.** Our teens
  need to know what a healthy

relationship actually looks like. Give an example of your own marriage, a strong friendship, or any other relationship that displays healthy qualities.

- **Using their voice.** Your child has a voice; encourage them to use it. If they are uncomfortable, it's important to voice that in the moment rather than staying silent.

- **Consent.** We talked about this in the last section, and it's an important one to revisit. Our kids need to have a solid definition of consent so they can protect themselves if a situation arises with the potential for assault.

Let your child know that they can always be honest with you—especially if someone has told them to keep something a secret.

WHAT DO I DO IF MY CHILD HAS BEEN SEXUALLY ASSAULTED?

BELIEVE THEM.

They're likely feeling a great deal of guilt and shame, even though the assault was not their fault or within their control. If your child comes to you with something sensitive like this, it's important to make sure they're heard and commended for sharing it with you. The best response you can give is letting them know you have full confidence in their word, even if they say someone you love or trust has done something inappropriate.[5]

Note: There are some cases, though few and far between, in which someone wrongfully accuses someone else in an effort to hurt them or their reputation. If you're not sure that your child can be trusted *or* if you find it hard to believe that the accused would behave thus, you still owe it to your child to investigate their claims and keep them away from

The best response you can give is letting them know you have full confidence in their word, even if they say someone you love or trust has done something inappropriate.

the accused, even if you can never be fully sure what happened. It's not worth taking the risk that they were, in fact, telling the truth. You know your child better than anyone. If they are sincere and trustworthy in other situations, you can be confident they are telling the truth in this situation.

BE STRONG.

This may seem like a lot to ask of a parent who's just heard such shocking news, but it is exactly what your child needs. If they've been left in a vulnerable, scary place, they'll need you more than ever. *Your child is counting on you for support.* It's normal to feel angry, shocked, anxious, helpless, or fearful if your child comes to you with this.[6] But now is an important time to process your emotions as best you can so that you can be the support your kids need.

REAFFIRM THEIR WORTH.

Affirm in your child that they're loved and brave for bringing this to you. They may feel like "damaged goods," so assure them that assault has not changed who they are in the slightest. As parents, it's our job to remind our kids of who they are in times of doubt, and sexual assault does not reflect poorly on the victim's character; it only reflects poorly on the offender. We want our kids to see their value in every way, despite how low they may feel after a traumatizing assault.

TELL THEM THEY'RE SAFE.

Our children need to know they're safe from harm. *Assure your child that you will do everything you can to protect them.* After experiencing a sexual assault, it's hard to know whom to trust or how to move on from such deep pain. Everything your child knows about their world has

As parents, it's our job
to remind our kids of
who they are in times of
doubt, and sexual assault
does not reflect poorly
on the victim's character;
it only reflects poorly on
the offender.

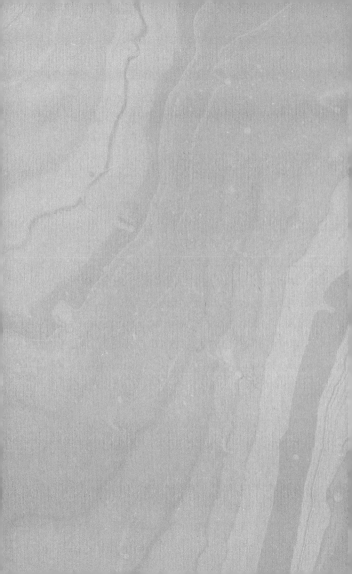

been turned upside down, and it's frightening. Tell your child that you won't let any more harm come to them. They did the right thing in telling you about it, and you will do everything in your power to keep them safe.

GET HELP.

We encourage you to take proper legal action against the offender.[7] It's important to contact the local police.[8] This may seem intimidating to you or your child, but take comfort in knowing that specially trained officers will be able to guide you through the process every step of the way.

Also consider calling the National Sexual Assault Hotline at 800-656-HOPE (4673). This hotline will direct you to speak with someone from your local sexual assault service provider.

If your child has been sexually abused, you may observe changes in behavior such as sleeplessness, appetite loss, aggression, depressive symptoms, self-harm, or other major changes.[9] We can offer our children all the love and support we can, but if these signs persist it may be time to seek further help. Talk with your child about seeing a counselor. Therapy may seem scary to them, so make sure they understand the helpful tools it can offer for sexual assault survivors.

WHAT DO I DO IF MY CHILD IS ACCUSED OF (OR CONFESSES TO) COMMITTING SEXUAL ASSAULT?

BUILD TRUST.

A child who has been accused of sexual assault may feel confused by the situation. If your child is very young, they may not realize that what they did was inappropriate. If they don't understand why they've been accused of something—or if they do understand, but fear the consequences—they likely won't know whom they can trust. As a result of this fear, the child may not disclose every detail or be completely honest about the facts of the situation.

Tell your child that you want to help them but can only do so if they are completely open about what happened. When appropriate, use it as a teachable moment (such as a five-year-old child who unknowingly looks at or touches another child's private areas).[10] Rather than saying, "don't do this," talk about *why* it's inappropriate.

TELL THEM THAT YOU LOVE THEM.

If your child regrets something he or she has done, the emotions to come are surely going to feel burdensome. But first and foremost, we need our kids to know that we love them *no matter what*. Tell them what they've done was wrong, but clearly state that you love them and will walk with them as they face the consequences.

GET HELP.

As hard as this situation is, a child is not likely to outgrow inappropriate sexual behavior over time without help. Family therapy is a good way to start healing conversations. If your child is not ready for family therapy, you may consider individual counseling for them instead. Either way, they're likely working through emotions of shame and guilt, and counseling will help them face those in a healthy

First and foremost, we need our kids to know that we love them no matter what.

way. It is also highly possible that, if your child abused someone, he or she may have been a victim of abuse in the past. Therapy and intense counseling can get to the root of the problem and hopefully provide healing and restoration.

HELP THEM SEEK RECONCILIATION AND FORGIVENESS.

Simply confessing to you is not enough; God is clear that we need to confess our sins to those whom we've sinned against, and your child needs to do so as well.[11] It's scary, humiliating, and painful, but true repentance also leads to restoration, freedom, and healing—for both your child and the victim.

First, help them put themselves in the other person's shoes and feel what they might have felt. Ask how they would feel if someone did that to them. Once they've confronted this, give them time to process and grieve their actions. When they're ready, go with them to apologize. Show that you'll never give up on them, even when they sin—just as Christ fought for us while we were yet sinners.[12] Later, help your child process their apology. Remind them that even if the person didn't forgive them in the moment, your child needs to do what God asks of them, regardless of the other person's reaction.

ENFORCE NEW BOUNDARIES.

As part of the process, you need to calmly but firmly explain to your child that because they sinned, they will face consequences. (The form those consequences take is up to you.) One of the main goals of these consequences is reestablishing trust and responsibility. Remind them that you're doing this because you love them and want what's best for them.

WHAT DOES GOD'S WORD SAY ABOUT SEXUAL ASSAULT?

THE OLD TESTAMENT IS PRETTY CLEAR about God's view on sexual assault and how to act when boundaries have been crossed. Let's start with Deuteronomy 22:23-29. Deuteronomy is full of laws for God's people, and this section of text protects women in particular against assault.[13] The passage gives three possible scenarios:

1. *If a man has sex with a virgin woman engaged to be married, they should both be stoned to death.* The man deserves death because he slept with a woman promised to another man. The woman deserves death because she did not cry for help even though she was in a town (i.e., a place where her cries would be heard), which indicates that she was a willing participant.

2. *If a man rapes an engaged woman, he should be stoned to death while she is protected from harm.* Scripture

compares this scenario to someone who commits murder. The man found the woman out in the country and forced her to have sex with him (she screamed but was not heard), so it is considered rape. He pays a price, but she is protected.

3. *If a man has sex with a woman not engaged to be married, he has to pay the dowry, marry her, and never divorce her.* The wording is a bit different in this verse: it says that they are "discovered" (Deuteronomy 22:28), which implies some form of mutual responsibility that's different from the previous scenario. But the man is still held responsible because he is the one who initiated the sexual encounter. The fact that he's required to marry this woman means she is now under his care and he must provide for her.

It's important to note the language used in each of these scenarios. God's Word differentiates between sexual immorality and rape. Sexual immorality places responsibility on both man and woman, while rape is solely blamed on the perpetrator. God makes it clear that in cases of assault, a price must be paid and the victim is not to blame. Our God is a God of justice and mercy: justice for the offender and mercy for the innocent. God sees the woman who's been attacked and values her enough to save her from any shame. She is not shunned for what's happened to her because it was out of her control. In fact, her reputation is restored in full. She is not to be used for a man's pleasure and quickly discarded; God's law is meant to protect her. When our children are hurt our merciful Father tenderly cares for them and sees when they're in distress.

Though this law was in place, 2 Samuel 13 shows that sinful human nature persisted—as it does today. Amnon, son of King David, was in love with his half sister Tamar. In a conniving scheme, he tricked Tamar into tending to him while he was "sick." When she arrived to help, he overcame her despite her cries. He wasn't really sick after all. After violating Tamar, Amnon actually *hated* her—yes, his feelings changed quickly from love to hatred—and ordered her out of his home. Scripture says she lived as a "desolate woman" after that (2 Samuel 13:20). Amnon had broken God's law, causing Tamar to suffer.

One of the saddest parts of this story is that Tamar's brother Absalom told her to keep silent about the incident. Absalom took revenge by killing Amnon (which could be argued also served his own

If your child has been the victim of others' lusts, this God knows every tear they've cried, every pain they've felt, and He's taken it all upon Himself through the Cross.

purposes, since the two men were vying for King David's throne), while Tamar was left with the repercussions. People don't often get it right, but God promises to "[heal] the brokenhearted."[14] He sees us in our pain, even when the world around us seems to turn its back.

So what can we learn from Tamar? We can use the pain we see in this story to learn how to love our children more tenderly than Tamar was loved. There are also two important characteristics to observe in Tamar.[15] First, she knew right from wrong. There was no question that she knew what Amnon demanded was inappropriate. She actually tried to convince him to propose marriage to her rather than force himself on her. We need our children to be outspoken and clear about their boundaries as well. Second, she has a strong voice. Tamar does not stay quiet while this is happening. She yells out repeatedly, telling Amnon of the dishonor he'd be committing. Sadly, she was eventually overcome, but she exercised the power of her voice. Our sons and daughters have a voice too, and we should encourage them to use it, even when they feel helpless. You never know when someone's protest might make the difference.

Sin, dysfunction, and pain flourish in silence and isolation, and Satan knows it. He knows how vulnerable we are when we feel like outcasts, unworthy, defiled, and unlovable. The enemy loves darkness because that's where he can make our secrets, shame, and hurt torment our every thought. But when we begin to step into the light, Satan is no match for the redeeming power of Jesus. Ephesians 5:8-16 tells us that we're children of light.

Everything exposed by the light becomes visible. Fear, guilt, depression, and pain have no place to hide in the light of the Lord. This exposure can only lead to life, forgiveness, and restored joy. As scary as it is to speak up, we need to. And we need to help our kids feel safe enough to do the same.

Perhaps most important, God's Word talks clearly and frequently about how He protects the meek, the downtrodden, the mourners, the orphan, the widow, those in distress, the "alien" (i.e., the immigrant or refugee), the helpless, the victim, the sinner... He desires that *none* should perish,[16] that *all* should come to repentance. He also says that He hates wrongdoing and loves justice,[17] and that vengeance is His.[18] As you equip your kids to resist those who would harm them and to discern right from wrong, also remind them of exactly who is on their side, fighting for them tirelessly and ceaselessly.

If your child has been the victim of others' lusts, this God knows every tear they've cried, every pain they've felt, and He's taken it all upon Himself through the Cross. He's with them through it all, He's *for* them, and He desires that they once again flourish in His love. Help them learn to forgive their abuser, knowing full well that God will bring about true justice in His perfect timing.

If your child has been accused of or has committed an assault, take heart. Your child is *not* beyond God's grace and redemption; he or she is included in the "all" whom God desires to come to repentance, and He is working toward that end goal. Continue to pray for your child, speak truth over them, and shower them in love—but also allow them to experience consequences for their actions. Help them become the image-bearer God desires them to be. And remember that only God can turn helpless situations into stories of beauty, redemption, forgiveness, and flourishing.

HOW DO I TEACH MY CHILDREN TO RESPECT THE SEXUAL DIGNITY OF OTHERS?

To respect other people's sexual dignity, we first need to be empathetic toward their emotions and opinions. This means being aware of how a person is feeling and why they feel that way—and responding respectfully.

- **Discuss empathy.** To respect other people's sexual dignity, we first need to be empathetic toward their emotions and opinions. This means being aware of how a person is feeling and why they feel that way—and responding respectfully.

- **Talk about expressing emotions.** If we want others to be empathetic toward us, we need to be willing to share our feelings too. Boys in particular need to know that manliness does not mean aggression. Our boys should know that it's okay to share their emotions, express when they're upset, and find healthy outlets for their feelings. This will translate to relationships with the opposite sex because it shows them how to have open communication (whether it's with a friend or a significant other).

- **Define sexual harassment and encourage them to speak up.**[19] We want our kids to learn how to recognize when something inappropriate is happening and actually speak up. For example, if a student places his hand on a girl's leg in class without her permission, it's considered sexual harassment. Let's raise vocal kids who speak up when something isn't right.

- **Teach your sons to be moral leaders.** Whether it's politicians, athletes, or celebrities, "bro culture" has created an environment in which wealthy and powerful men believe they are entitled to a woman's body. *They are not.* Model appropriate speech and behavior for them to follow. There's never an excuse for "locker-room talk."

Encourage them to be an ethical voice to confront and call out inappropriate speech and behavior among their friends.

DISCUSSION QUESTIONS

1. How would you define "consent"?

2. What does our culture say about sexual assault?

3. Can you think of an example of sexual assault? Or do you know someone who has experienced sexual assault?

4. If you witnessed harassment, what would you do?

5. How can you be a friend to someone who's gone through sexual assault?

6. What are some ways you can protect yourself from sexual assault?

7. What do you think about the sexual violence you see on TV or in movies? Is it okay to watch this kind of content? Why or why not?

8. How can you act respectfully toward guys/girls?

9. What do you think defines a healthy relationship?

10. How can you establish good boundaries in a relationship?

11. How can I be a safe haven for you?

12. Do you feel comfortable coming to me with anything, including something you think might be wrong or bad? If not, how can I help you feel more comfortable?

RECAP

- Sexual assault is any form of sexual contact or behavior that occurs without the consent of the victim.

- "Consent" is verbal permission. If this is not present, it's assault.

- We need to start conversations about sexual assault when our kids are young so we can raise them to protect themselves and others from harm.

- If your child has been sexually assaulted, believe them, be strong, reaffirm their worth, tell them they're safe, and get help.

- If your child is accused of sexual assault, build trust, tell them you love them, get help, help them seek reconciliation and forgiveness, and enforce new boundaries.

- The Bible shows both what *to do* and what *not to do* when it comes to sexual assault. God sees the sexual dignity of His people, which is why His law includes clear consequences for offenders and protection for the abused. In Tamar's story, we see that human sin can deeply hurt the lives of others.

- The Bible also shows us how to distinguish right from wrong in sexual situations, and that we all have a voice—so we should use it!

- Teaching our kids about the sexual dignity of other people starts with empathy and caring for the feelings of others. We want to instill strong values in our kids so they can grow up to pursue healthy relationships.

- We need to model for our kids what healthy relationships look like.

Teaching our kids about the sexual dignity of other people starts with empathy and caring for the feelings of others.

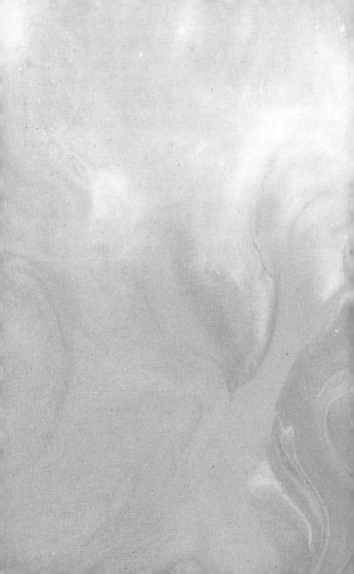

FINAL THOUGHTS

THE #METOO MOVEMENT has spurred a chain reaction over the past few years.[20] It advocates that "you are not alone," and that's the same message we want to show our kids every day. From the small parts of their lives, like hearing about their soccer practice or art project at school, to the big parts, like talking about faith and relationships, we need our kids to know that they're *never* alone.

Sexual assault is scary, but there are ways we can prepare ourselves as parents to make it less likely—starting with honesty and ending with love. When our kids feel safe to verbalize, process, and emote, they'll know whom they can turn to in times of need. We must pray for our kids daily, not only that they will remain safe from harm, but that they will continue to grow in the love we model for them and to stand up for others who need support.

Sexual assault is scary, but there are ways we can prepare ourselves as parents to make it less likely—starting with honesty and ending with love.

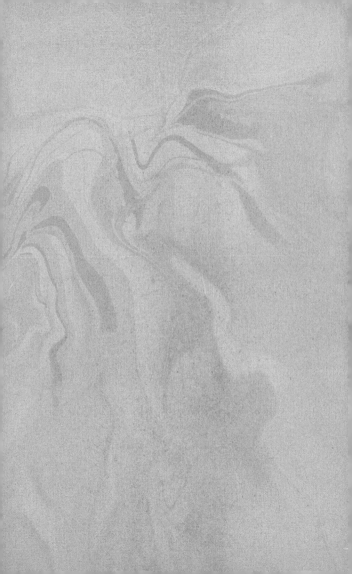

ADDITIONAL RESOURCES

1. Kristen A. Jenson (of Defend Young Minds, https://www.defendyoungminds.com/), *Good Pictures Bad Pictures* (for ages 7+) and *Good Pictures Bad Pictures Jr.* (for ages 3-6). These books are more specifically about pornography, but their techniques for bringing up inappropriate images can transfer over to talking about sexual assault.

2. Korin Miller, "What Is Sexual Assault (and What Isn't), according to the Law," *Self*, https://www.self.com/story/sexual-assault-definition

3. Gorana Hitrec, "Teaching Children to Protect Themselves from Sexual Abuse," http://docplayer.net/21613559-12-teaching-children-to-protect-themselves-from-sexual-abuse.html

4. "What Should I Do after a Child Tells?" Stop It Now!, https://www.stopitnow.org/ohc-content/what-should-i-do-after-a-child-tells

5. "Tips for Talking with Survivors of Sexual Assault," RAINN, https://www.rainn.org/articles/tips-talking-survivors-sexual-assault

6. "Talking to Your Kids about Sexual Assault," RAINN, https://www.rainn.org/articles/talking-your-kids-about-sexual-assault

7. "Help for Parents of Children Who Have Been Sexually Abused by Family Members," RAINN, https://www.rainn.org/articles/help-parents-children-who-have-been-sexually-abused-family-members

8. Ruth Everhart, "Women of the Bible say #MeToo," *Christian Century*, https://www.christiancentury.org/article/critical-essay/women-bible-say-metoo

9. Jaimie Seaton, "What to Do When Your Child Is Accused of Sexually Inappropriate Behavior," *Washington Post*, https://www.washingtonpost.com/lifestyle/2018/10/25/what-do-when-your-child-is-accused-sexually-inappropriate-behavior/

10. "Families of Juvenile Sex Offenders," American Association for Marriage and Family Therapy, https://www.aamft.org/Consumer_Updates/Families_of_Juvenile_Sex_Offenders.aspx

NOTES

1. "Child Sexual Abuse Statistics," National Center for Victims of Crime, accessed September 29, 2022, https://victimsofcrime .org/child-sexual-abuse-statistics/.

2. Korin Miller, "What Is Sexual Assault (and What Isn't), according to the Law," *Self*, November 3, 2017, https://www.self.com/story/sexual -assault-definition.

3. "Perpetrators of Sexual Violence: Statistics," RAINN, accessed September 21, 2022, https:// www.rainn.org/statistics/perpetrators-sexual -violence.

4. "The Underwear Rule," Council of Europe, accessed September 21, 2022, https://www .coe.int/en/web/children/underwear-rule.

5. "What Should I Do after a Child Tells?" Stop It Now!, accessed September 21, 2022, https:// www.stopitnow.org/ohc-content/what -should-i-do-after-a-child-tells.

6. "Help for Parents of Children Who Have Been Sexually Abused by Family Members," RAINN, accessed September 21, 2022, https://www

.rainn.org/articles/help-parents-children-who
-have-been-sexually-abused-family-members.

7. "Childhelp National Child Abuse Hotline,"
   accessed September 21, 2022, https://
   childhelphotline.org/.

8. "Sexual Assault and Teenagers," Raising
   Children.net.au, accessed September 21,
   2022, https://raisingchildren.net.au/teens
   /mental-health-physical-health/sexual
   -assault-sexual-abuse/sexual-assault.

9. "Tip Sheet: Warning Signs of Possible Sexual
   Abuse in a Child's Behaviors," Stop It Now!,
   accessed September 21, 2022, https://www
   .stopitnow.org/ohc-content/warning-signs
   -possible-abuse.

10. Jaimie Seaton, "What to Do When Your
    Child Is Accused of Sexually Inappropriate
    Behavior," *Washington Post*, October 25, 2018,
    https://www.washingtonpost.com/lifestyle
    /2018/10/25/what-do-when-your-child-is
    -accused-sexually-inappropriate-behavior
    /?utm_term=.61d32cb940f5.

11. James 5:16

12. Romans 5:8

13. Katie McCoy, "What Does the Bible Say about Sexual Assault?" The Ethics & Religious Liberty Commission, March 10, 2015, https://erlc.com /resource-library/articles/what-does-the -bible-say-about-sexual-assault/.

14. Psalm 147:3

15. Ruth Everhart, "Women of the Bible Say #MeToo," *Christian Century*, July 17, 2018, https://www.christiancentury.org/article /critical-essay/women-bible-say-metoo.

16. 2 Peter 3:9

17. Isaiah 61:8

18. Deuteronomy 32:35; Romans 12:17-19

19. Catherine Thorbecke, "Raising Good Men: How Parents Can Teach Sons about Healthy Relationships and Consent," ABC News, December 19, 2017, https://abcnews.go.com /Lifestyle/raising-good-men-parents-teach -sons-healthy-relationships/story?id=51870168.

20. "Me Too.," accessed September 21, 2022, https://metoomvmt.org/.

PARENT GUIDES TO SOCIAL MEDIA
BY AXIS

It's common to feel lost in your teen's world. Let these be your go-to guides on social media, how it affects your teen, and how to begin an ongoing conversation about faith that matters.

BUNDLE THESE 5 BOOKS AND SAVE

PARENT GUIDES TO FINDING TRUE IDENTITY
BY AXIS

When culture is constantly pulling teens away from Christian values, let these five parent guides spark an ongoing conversation about finding your true identity in Christ.

BUNDLE THESE 5 BOOKS AND SAVE

www.axis.org

CP1814

PARENT GUIDES TO MENTAL & SEXUAL HEALTH
BY AXIS

Don't let mainstream media be the only voice in your teens' conversations about mental and sexual health. Gain confidence and unravel your fears about breaching these sensitive topics today.

BUNDLE THESE 5 BOOKS AND SAVE

www.axis.org

CP1846